I0429757

Inclusion or Exclusion of CEDAW's Concluding Observations on Health in Government Plans?

The case of South Asia

Ranjani.K.Murthy

Table of Contents

Acknowledgement

The author is grateful to women and men, health providers and women's health activists in South Asia with whom I have exchanged ideas on gender inequalities in health.

She is also grateful to Asia-Pacific Resource and Research Center for Women with whom she was associated between 2008 and 2011.

Lastly, I am thankful to my friends from Tamil Nadu, India for their solidarity and encouragement.

However, none of them bear any responsibility for shortcomings of this short book

Ranjani.K.Murthy
2014

Abbreviations

AIDS	Acquired Immunodeficiency Syndrome
ANC	Ante-Natal Care
CEDAW	Committee on the Elimination of All Forms of Discrimination against Women
DTP	Diphtheria, Tetanus, and Poliomyelitis
GDP	Gross Domestic Product
HIV	Human Immunodeficiency Virus
MCH	Maternal and Child Health
MDGs	Millennium Development Goals
MMR	Maternal Mortality Ratio
PNC	Post-Natal Care
PPP	Purchasing Power Parity
SRH	Sexual and Reproductive Health
UN	United Nations
UNICEF	United Nations Children's Fund
WHO	World Health Organisation

1.0 Introduction

The Convention on the Elimination of All Forms of Discrimination against Women (referred to as the Convention in this paper) was adopted in 1979 by the United Nations General Assembly and entered into force in 1981. It consists of a preamble and 30 Articles, of which Article 12 directly pertains to non-discrimination in health and four other Articles[1] touch upon women's health in the context of other sectors or issues (UN Women, n.d).

Article 12 emphasises the following two roles for the state so as to end discrimination against women:

1. States Parties shall take all appropriate measures to eliminate discrimination against women in the field of health care in order to ensure, on a basis of equality of men and women, access to health care services, including those related to family planning.

2. Notwithstanding the above provision, States Parties shall ensure to women appropriate services in connection with pregnancy, confinement and the post-natal period, granting free services where necessary, as well as adequate nutrition during pregnancy and lactation (UN Women, n.d)

---

[1] Article 10 pertaining to Education, Article 11 focusing on Employment, Article 14 pertaining to Rural Women and Article 16 on Marriage and Family Life (UN Women, n.d).

Article 10 of the Convention, with a focus on eliminating discrimination against women in education, mentions that State Parties should ensure that women have access to educational information to ensure the health and well-being of families, including information and advice on family planning. Article 11 with a focus on non-discrimination in employment, emphasizes State's duty to further women's right to health and to safety in working conditions, including the safeguarding of the function of reproduction. Article 14 on Rural Women refers to State responsibility to ensure rural women's access to adequate health care facilities, counseling and family planning services. Article 16 on Marriage and Family Life emphasizes that State should ensure that women have the same right as men in entering into marriage, choosing a spouse, deciding freely and responsibly on the number and spacing of their children and to have access to the information, education and means to enable them to exercise these rights (UN Women, n.d)

In 1999, the General Recommendation 24 on Women and Health was framed[2] by the Committee on the Elimination of All Forms of Discrimination against Women (CEDAW) [3] which monitors implementation of the Convention by State Parties (WHO, 2007). The General Recommendation clarifies that by the term discrimination against women in heath it means against both women and girls. Importantly it points out the following:

---

[2] It drew upon insights from the 1993 World Conference on Human Rights, the 1994 International Conference on Population and Development and the 1995 Fourth World Conference on Women and General Recommendations on other Articles of the Convention

[3] The CEDAW was established in 1982. It consists of 23 members with expertise in international women's human rights, who serve in their personal capacity. Members are elected by States Parties in a secret ballot, with due regard to equitable geographical representation and diversity of legal systems and cultural backgrounds (WHO, 2007).

- States parties should give special attention to health of women from vulnerable groups including migrant, refugee and international displaced women, the girl child and older women, women in prostitution, indigenous women and women with mental or physical disabilities.
- State parties should ensure non-discrimination in access in access of women to the social determinants of health, including water, sanitation, shelter, nutrition and safe working conditions. .
- Lack of services and protocols, by law or otherwise, to treat conditions and illnesses specific to or faced more by women should be considered discrimination against women. These could be linked with menstruation, pregnancy, menopause, incomplete abortions, violence against women (including sexual abuse, female genital mutilation), depression & post natal depression and with anorexia and bulimia. It recommends that punitive action against women who undergo abortion should be removed.
- State parties to report on implementation of health legislation, policies and plans for women. It should also report on whether privacy and confidentiality areas maintained while treating women[4], and whether services are provided without requiring authorization of husbands, parents and partners. Barriers such as high user fees, distance of facilities, and costs of transport should be removed. State should fund SRH health services for women.
- State parties should enact laws (including prohibiting early marriage, violence against women, polygamy, marital rape), formulate polices and health protocols to deal with[5] gender based violence, arranging of gender-sensitive training for health providers on handling cases of violence against women. States should not permit forced sterilization and testing for HIV

(CEDAW, 1999)

---

[4]The General Recommendation maintains that privacy is important In-particular for diseases of genital tract, contraception, incomplete abortion and injuries due to physical/sexual violence.
[5] Trauma treatment and counseling

The CEDAW is to review State reports on implementation of the Convention[6], review shadow reports from non-governmental actors, receive complaints from groups and individuals within the jurisdiction (if the State has signed the Optional Protocol), and then make Concluding Observations on important achievements and any issue affecting women to which it believes the States Parties should devote more attention to (WHO, 2007). **This paper seeks to examine whether the South Asian governments have taken the Concluding Observations pertaining to Health into account in the national planning process (five year plans and national development plans).**

The paper is structured as follows. The second section examines the reservations placed by different South Asian States while ratifying CEDAW. The third section analyses existing data on health and gender discrimination in health in South Asia. The fourth section explores how far the latest national development plans of South Asian countries incorporate the latest Concluding Observations of the CEDAW Committee on health. The paper concludes by examining whether national development plans of South Asian government include or exclude Concluding Observations on Health, and offers recommendations on how governments could be made more accountable to incorporate suggestions from Concluding Observations pertaining to national plans.

---

[6]The State parties are to report within a year after ratification/accession and thereafter every four years

2.0 Ratification and Reservations: The South Asian Context

Following United Nations Development Programme, South Asia includes the following eight countries: Afghanistan, Bangladesh, Bhutan, India, Maldives, Nepal, Pakistan and Sri Lanka (Kumar, 2010). All the South Asian countries have signed[7] or/and ratified[8]/acceded[9] to the Convention, with the first one to do so being Bhutan on 31/8/1981, and the last one being Afghanistan nearly twenty two years later on 02/03/2003. Details on reservation on the Convention and its Optional Protocol by the South Asian governments are given in Table 1.

Table 1: **Ratification and Declaration on Convention**

---

[7] Signature' of a treaty is an act by which a State provides a preliminary endorsement of the instrument. Signing does not create a legal obligation to abide by the treaty (UNICEF, n.d)

[8] 'Ratification' is an act by which a State signifies an agreement to be legally bound by the terms of a particular treaty. To ratify a treaty, the State first signs it and then fulfils its own constitutional procedures and makes a formal decision to be a party to the treaty (UNICEF, n.d).

[9] Accession' is an act by which a State signifies its agreement to be legally bound by the terms of a particular treaty. It has the same legal effect as ratification, but is not preceded by an act of signature (UNICEF, n.d).

Country	Reservations and Declarations	Text of Reservation and Declaration	Withdrawal of Reservation and Declaration	Whether and when signed or ratified/acceded to Optional Protocol
Afghanistan	None			Not ratified
Bangladesh	Reservation to Articles 2 , 13(1)(a), 16(1)(c)(f)	**Reservations**: The Bangladesh government does not consider as binding upon itself the provisions of Articles 2, 13 (a) and 16 (1) (c) and (f) as they conflict with Sharia law based on Holy Quran and Sunna.	**Withdrawal of reservation 13 (a) and 16(1)(f)**:On 23 July 1997	Signed and ratified on 6/9/2000
Bhutan	None			Not signed or ratified
India	Reservation to Article – 29(1); Declaration Art 5(a) &16(1),(2),	**Declarations**: i) With regard to Articles 5 (a) and 16 (1) of the Convention, the Indian government declares that it shall abide by and ensure these provisions in conformity with its policy of non-interference in the personal affairs of any Community without its consent. ii) With regard to Article 16 (2) of the Convention the Indian government declares that though in principle it fully supports the principle of compulsory registration of marriages, it is not practical in a vast country like India with its variety		Not signed or ratified

		of customs, religions and level of literacy. **Reservation**: With regard to Article 29 of the Convention the Indian Government declares that it does not consider itself bound by paragraph 1		
Maldives	Reservation to Articles – Art 7(a) & 16.	Reservations: The Government of Maldives will comply with the provisions of the Convention, except those which the Government may consider contradictory to the principles of the Islamic Sharia upon which the laws and traditions of the Maldives is founded. The Government of the Republic of Maldives expresses its reservation to article 7(a) of the Convention, to the extent that the provision contained in the said paragraph conflicts with the Constitution	Withdrawal of Reservation 7(a) –On 31 March 2010, the Government of withdrew its reservation regarding Article 7(a).	Date of ratification 13/03/2006
Nepal	None			Signed: 2001, Ratified 15//6/2007

Country	Reservations and Declarations	Text of Reservation and Declaration	Withdrawal of Reservation and Declaration	Whether and when signed or ratified/ acceded to Optional Protocol
Pakistan	Reservation to Article – 29(1) ; general declaration on accession subject to Constitutional provisions	**Declaration**: The accession by [the] Government of Pakistan to the Convention is subject to the provisions of its Constitution **Reservation**: The Government of Pakistan declares that it does not consider itself bound by paragraph 1 of Article 29 of the Convention.		Not signed
Sri Lanka	None			Ratified: 15 Oct 2002

Source: United Nations, n.da, UN, n.db, UN Women, n.d

Four out of eight countries ratified/acceded to the Convention without declarations[10] or reservations[11], namely Afghanistan, Bhutan, Nepal and Sri Lanka). Of the countries which placed a declaration or reservation (Bangladesh, India, Maldives, Pakistan), Bangladesh withdrew two out of three reservations on July 23, 1997.   India has placed the maximum number of declaration/reservations while ratifying/acceding to the Convention!

---

[10] A State may make a declaration about its understanding of a matter contained in or the interpretation of a particular provision in a treaty. Declarations do not purport to exclude or modify the legal effects of a

Pertaining to the Convention as a whole, the Government of Pakistan has declared that it accedes to Convention subject to the provisions of its Constitution. The Government of Maldives has reserved that will comply with the provisions of the Convention, except those which the Government may consider contradictory to the principles of the Islamic Sharia and traditions of Maldives. The Reservation is problematic as some practices under Sharia discriminate against women's physical or/and mental health such as permitting polygamy and flogging of women suspected of adultery.

If one analyses from Table 1 the declarations and reservations placed by South Asian governments on individual Articles, the following picture emerges:

- Article 2 states that **States Parties should condemn discrimination against women in all its forms, agree to pursue by all appropriate means and without delay a policy of eliminating discrimination against women. The Government of Bangladesh has reserved that** it does not consider as binding upon itself the provisions of Articles 2, as they conflict with Sharia law based on Holy Quran and Sunna. This reservation on an overarching Article which underpins the Convention has a direct bearing on elimination of discrimination pertaining to women's health, as well as various social determinants of women's health

- Article 5 (a) relates to **elimination of prejudices and customary and all other practices which are based on the idea of the inferiority or the superiority of either of the sexes** The Indian government has Declared that it shall abide by and ensure provisions of Articles 5 (a) of the Convention but it conformity

treaty (Asian Legal Research Center, n.d).
[11] Reservations are any statement made upon signature, ratification, or accession to a treaty which purports to exclude or modify the legal effect of a treaty (Asian Legal Research Center, n.d)

with its policy of non-interference in the personal affairs of any Community without its consent. This Article is indeed central to elimination of discrimination in the field of health in India, as practices such as women eating last and least, early marriage, menstrual taboos, forced marriage, and devadasi system persist in the country.

- Article 7 (a) emphasises women's right to vote in all elections and public referenda and to be eligible for election to all publicly elected bodies. The Government of Maldives has reserved that it will adhere to this Article to the extent that the provision contained in the said paragraph conflicts with the Constitution. There is evidence that more the proportion of women in elected bodies the greater the accountability to deliver health services for women and address social determinants (Bahuguna, 2010)

- Article 16 (1) recommends that States Parties should take all appropriate measures to eliminate discrimination against women in matters relating to marriage and family relations. Like in case of Articles 5 (a) the Indian government declares that it shall abide by and ensure these provisions in conformity with its policy of non-interference in the personal affairs of any Community without its consent.

- Article 16 (2) states all necessary action, including legislation, shall be taken to specify a minimum age for marriage and to make the registration of marriages in an official registry compulsory. The Indian government has declared that compulsory registration of marriages was not practical in a vast country like India with its variety of customs, religions and level of literacy. This makes it difficult to prevent early marriage and affects adolescent health, including reproductive and sexual health and rights

- Paragraph 1 of Article 29 of the Convention empowers the International Court of Justice to intervene if arbitration is not possible in the event of a dispute between two or more States Parties concerning the interpretation or application of the present

Convention. The Government of Pakistan and India have placed a reservation stating that it does not consider itself bound by (1)

As mentioned, Optional Protocol to the Convention allows individuals and groups to place their complaints (pertaining to the implementation of Convention by their country) before the Committee. However, for this to be actually possible, the concerned government should have signed the Optional Protocol. As of 21st May, 2014, only four out of eight countries had signed and ratified or ratified the Optional Protocol, namely Bangladesh, Nepal, Maldives and Sri Lanka. The remaining four have not ratified it in-spite of pressure from women's groups from within the country, as well as the CEDAW Committee.

3.0 Statistics on Health and Gender Discrimination in health in South Asia

This section examines data on health expenditure , health systems, risk factors, access to women's specific health services, and demographic & health outcomes (including gender disparities) in South Asia .

3.1 Understanding health expenditure

As per the World Health Statistics, 2013 total expenditure on health as a percent of Gross Domestic Product for the year 2010 ranged from a low 1.0% in the case of Pakistan to 10.4% in the case of Afghanistan. The comparable figure for the world as a whole stands at 9.2% of Gross Domestic Product, with only Afghanistan exceeding this figure and Sri Lanka recording two thirds the global average (WHO, 2013). See Table 2 for country-wise details.

The per capita total expenditure on health in PPP US$ varies from a low $10 in the case of Pakistan to a high $409 in the case of Maldives, an upper middle income country as of 2010 (WHO, 2013). The average global per-capita total expenditure on health stood at US$ 941 in 2010. In 2003, the Macro Economic Commission on Health estimated that a minimum of $34 per capita per annum in health is required to deliver essential health interventions (WHO,n da). In 2004 the Yemen government estimated that US$53 per capita is required to meet MDGs pertaining to Health by 2015. While the latter estimate may be specific to Yemen, it is a more realistic yardstick for what South Asian governments should aim at to meet the essential health services/MDGs on health, given that costs of health delivery have increased since 2003(WHO, N.db). Only three of the eight South Asian countries meet the Yemen estimate of total per capita expenditure on health per annum ($ 53) to achieve health MDGs (Maldives, Sri Lanka, and Bhutan). All South Asian governments other than Pakistan, Bangladesh and Nepal meet the Macro Economic Commission on Health's 2003 estimate of an investment of $34 per capita per annum in health to meet essential health services (WHO, 2013). See Table 2 for country-wise details.

Table 2: Health Expenditure in South Asia

Country	Total expenditure on health as % of GDP	Per capita total expenditure on health PPP int US$	Government expenditure on health as % of total expenditure on health	Private expenditure as a % of total expenditure on health	Government expenditure on health as % of total government expenditure	Social security expenditure on health as % of government expenditure on health
Year of data	2010	2010	2010	2010	2010	2010
Afghanistan	10.4	44	22.5	77.5	3.9	0
Bangladesh	3.7	25	36.5	63.5	8.9	0
Bhutan	4.3	89	84.6	15.4	8.4	0
India	3.7	51	28.2	74.8	6.8	19
Maldives	6.2	409	60.8	39.2	9.3	1
Nepal	5.1	28	37.4	62.6	9.5	4.1
Pakistan	1.0	10	76.6	23.4	3.4	3.4
Sri Lanka	3.5	82	45.6	54.4	6.9	0.1
Global	**9.2**	**941**	**58.9**	**41.1**	**15.1**	**60.1**

Source: WHO, 2013

An examination of the percentage of government/public and private expenditure on health as a percentage of total health expenditure as of 2010 reveals that private expenditure far exceeds public expenditure in Afghanistan, India, Bangladesh, Nepal and (recently) Sri Lanka (WHO, 2013). If one examines the global average it is the reverse. This reliance on private health expenditure in 5 out of 8 South Asian countries is problematic as out-of pocket expenditure constitutes a majority of private health expenditure, and not insurance. Women's earnings are lower than that of men in all south Asian countries (UNDP 2013). Women are not always able to exercise control over income, and incur debts to access health care for themselves and their family members. Further, private health sector rarely has a presence in remote and conflict ridden areas. Government expenditure is greater than private expenditure as of 2010 in the case of Bhutan, Pakistan and Maldives (WHO, 2013). Most of the government health expenditure in South Asia comes from taxes, and little through external aid or social security. The exception is Afghanistan where a little over quarter of government health expenditure comes from external resources. .

3.2 Health systems

Analysis of data from World Health Statistics, 2013 on number of staff and beds per 10,000 population, suggests that the number of community health workers, nurses & midwives, physicians, psychiatrists and beds per 10,000 population is lower than the global average in most of the South Asian countries for the period 2005-2012. See Table 3 for country-wise data.

Community health workers play an important role in transforming attitudes, as well as reaching services to girls and women where gender norms restrict their mobility. Data on community health workers per 10,000 population was available for four of the eight South Asian countries. It suggests the number of CHWs range from 0.5 per 10000 population in India to 13.8 in Maldives (as of 2005-12), with most other countries veering to the Indian average (WHO, 2013). Globally there are 29 nurses and midwives per 10,000 population as of 2005-12, and 5 of the 6 South Asian countries on which data was available fall short of this global average (other than Maldives at 44.5). This number is particularly low in Bangladesh at 2.2 and it is a concern as nurses/midwives are important for strengthening sexual and reproductive health services (including maternal health). The number of physicians per 10,000 population stands at 13.9 globally (as of 2005-12). None of the South Asian countries match this global average. Pakistan has the highest number of physicians- 8.1- at per 10000 population while Bhutan the least at 0.7 as of 2005-11.

The WHO estimates that countries with fewer than 23 health-care professionals (counting only physicians, nurses and midwives) per 10 000 population will be unlikely to achieve coverage rates for the key primary health-care interventions emphasised by MDGs (WHO, 2009). Except Maldives and Sri Lanka, none of the other South Asian countries have achieved the target as of 2005-12 (WHO, 2013).

Psychiatrists are important to address the growing problem of mental illnesses. None of the South Asian countries match the global average of 0.3 psychiatrists per 10000 population (for the period 2005-12). Maldives comes closest with 0.2 psychiatrists per 10000 population, with other countries having less than 0.05 psychiatrists for the same population. It is known that more women suffer from depression than men, and lack of adequate number of psychiatrists is problematic. Patel and Shindaye (n.d) argue that the increased risk of women in South Asia is both due to the harsher social environments for women (for example, their exposure to interpersonal violence) as well as reproductive and maternal factors (for example, post natal depression) (Patel and Shindaye. n.d).

The scenario with regard to number of beds per 100000 population is better. Globally there are 30 beds per 10000 population as of 2005-12, and in Nepal, Maldives and Sri Lanka there are more beds than the global average for the same population. Questions of where these beds are remain (mountains or plains, islands or mainland, in ethnic minority or majority dominated areas). However, in Afghanistan, Bangladesh, Pakistan and India there are less than 10 beds per 10000 population. See Table 3 for country wise details.

Table 3: Health Systems –South Asia

Country	CHWs per 10000 population	Nurses and midwives per 10000 population	Physicians per 10000 population	Psychiatrists per 10000 population	Beds per 10000 population
Year	2005-12	2005-12	2005-12	2005-12	2005-12
Afghanistan	ND	ND	1.9	<0.05	4
Bangladesh	3.3	2.2	3.6	<0.05	6
Bhutan	0.9	2.9	0.7	<0.05	18
India	0.5	10	6.5	<0.05	9
Maldives	13.8	44.5	16	0.20	43
Nepal	ND	ND	ND	<0.05	50
Pakistan	0.6	5.6	8.1	<0.05	6
Sri Lanka	ND	19.3	4.9	<0.05	36
Global	**ND**	**29**	**13.9**	**0.3**	**30**

Source: WHO, 2013

3.3 Risk factors

On a positive note, in all but one south Asian country-Afghanistan-more than 80% of the population has access to improved drinking water sources as of 2011 (WHO, 2013). Access to improved drinking water is comparable to global average of 89% in five South Asian countries (Bhutan, India, Maldives, Pakistan, and Sri Lanka. With greater access to improved drinking water, women's drudgery associated with fetching water reduces (UNICEF, n.d).

The situation with regard to proportion of population with access to improved sanitation as of 2011 is more dismal. Other than Maldives and Sri Lanka less than 62% of the population (global average) of the other South Asian countries have access to improved sanitation facilities (WHO, 2013). Lack of improved sanitation facilities affects women more than men as they find it difficult to use open defecation spaces during the day, and during the night it is not always safe to use open defecation spaces (UNICEF, n.d). Menstruation and pregnancy pose particular challenges to women when sanitation facilities are inadequate as they have to frequently use toilets. If one examines percentage of population still using solid fuels for cooking as of 2010, it is higher than the global average of 41% in all South Asian countries other than Maldives and Bhutan (WHO, 2013).   Using solid fuels poses health hazards for women – in particular respiratory infections- and there is a need to move towards sustainable and health friendly resources.

Table 4: Risk Factors Affecting Women's health

Country	% population using improved drinking water sources[12]	% using improved sanitation	% using solid fuels	Prevalence of raised fasting blood glucose among adults aged ≥ 25 years M F		Prevalence of raised blood pressure among adults aged ≥ 25 years M F	
Year	2011	2011	2010	2008		2008	
Afghanistan	61	28	85	8.9	9.5	1.5	3.3
Bangladesh	83	55	91	12.8	15.2	27.4	27.9
Bhutan	97	45	40	12	12.6	29	26.9
India	92	35	58	11.1	10.8	23.1	22.6
Maldives	99	98	8	7.8	7.5	30.6	24.5
Nepal	88	35	81	9.8	9.3	26.6	28.6
Pakistan	91	47	64	11.7	14.1	28.6	28.0
Sri Lanka	93	91	75	9.3	8.6	31	26.2
Global	**89**	**64**	**41**	**9.8**	**9.2**	**29.2**	**24.8**

Source: WHO, 2013

---

[12] Improved drinking water sources include: Piped water into dwelling, plot or yard, public tap/stand pipe, well/borehole, protected dug well, protected spring and rainwater collection (WHO, 2013)

Table 4 continued: Risk Factors Affecting Women's health

	Prevalence of smoking any tobacco product among adults aged ≥15 years (2009)		Population aged 15–24 years with comprehensive correct knowledge of HIV/AIDS		Prevalence of condom use by adults aged 15–49 years during higher risk sex	
			M	F		
					M	F
	M	F				
Year	2009		2005-2011		2011	
Afghanistan	ND	ND	ND	ND	ND	ND
Bangladesh	ND	ND	ND	ND	ND	ND
Bhutan	ND	ND	ND	ND	ND	ND
India	26	4	36	20	23	12
Maldives	43	11	ND	ND	ND	ND
Nepal	36	29	34	26	27	ND
Pakistan	34	6	ND	ND	ND	ND
Sri Lanka	27	ND	ND	ND	ND	ND
Global	36	8	ND	Nd	ND	ND

Source: WHO, 2013

Prevalence of raised fasting blood glucose is globally higher amongst men than women (aged 25 years and above) as of 2008 (WHO, 2013). However in four South Asian countries- Afghanistan, Bangladesh, Bhutan, and Pakistan- it is the reverse (See Table 4). Similarly, in contrast to the global trend, blood pressure is higher amongst women than men (aged 25 years and above) as of 2008 in Afghanistan, Bangladesh and Nepal. Higher level of stress amongst women than men and lesser ability to follow medical or exercise regime that is required to bring blood pressure or fasting blood glucose down is a constraint. On the positive side, data from World Health Statistics, 2013 prevalence of smoking and tobacco use is lower amongst women than men aged 15 and above as of 2009 in all South Asian Countries. However, the prevalence is higher than the global average for women in two out of four South Asian countries on which data was available. The high risk countries are Nepal and Maldives. The association between 29% prevalence of smoking amongst Nepali women and respiratory infections and maternal morbidity needs greater investigation. One study in Nepal does notes that the risks of maternal mortality was higher amongst smokers than non-smokers (Christian et al, 2004)

Data on population aged 15-24 years with comprehensive correct knowledge of HIV/AIDS was available from World Health Statistics, 2013 for only two South Asian countries, namely India and Nepal, and it reveals that more males had correct knowledge than females as of 2005-11 (WHO, 2013). The gender gap in awareness was particularly high in India. Related to HIV, is the issue of prevalence of condom use by those aged 15-49 years during higher risk sex. Data on this indicator was available only for India (for both sexes) and Nepal (only for males). Use of condom during higher risk sex is only 12% amongst females, and 23% amongst males in India. This suggests that women have lower negotiating power, as well as lesser availability of female condoms than male condoms. A greater proportion of men reported using condoms during higher risk sex in Nepal than in India (WHO, 2013). See Table 4 for country wise data.

3.4 <u>Access to gender just health laws and to health services</u>

<u>Health laws</u>
Approximately 25% of the world's population lives in countries with highly restrictive abortion laws (World on Waves, n.da).   Coming to South Asia, only in Nepal is abortion legally available on demand; other than for sex-selective abortion (World on Waves, n.db). In Afghanistan abortion is illegal under Article 402 of the Penal Code (Women on Waves, n.da). In Sri Lanka and Bangladesh, abortion is permitted only to save the lives of the pregnant women (Women on Waves, n.dc, n.dd).   However menstrual regulation is permitted in health facilities in Bangladesh. In Maldives abortion is legally available to save the lives of the pregnant women or preserve her physical health (UN, n.d c). In Pakistan abortion is allowed to save the lives of women, to preserve mental health and in instances of rape (World on Waves, n.de).   There is no law prohibiting sex-selective abortion. In Bhutan abortion is available for similar reasons as Pakistan and in addition in instances of incest (World on Waves, n.df). In India abortion is available on grounds similar to Bhutan, and in addition foetal impairment and economic-social conditions of the women (World on Waves, n.dg, UN.n.dd).   Like Nepal, sex-selective abortions illegal in India (Government, of India, 1994).

Unsafe and clandestine abortion adversely affects women's health, and can lead to maternal death. At the same time, sex selective abortion is a health issue as repeated pregnancies affects the physical, reproductive and mental health of women pressurised to undergo sex selective abortion. Further, reduction in sex ratio at birth has a bearing on increase in violence against women.

Information on legislations to punish acts of various forms of domestic violence[13] against women was available for six South Asian countries (other than Afghanistan and Maldives) from the Global Gender Gap Report, 2013. It rates the legislations on a scale of 0 to 1, with 1 being the worst score and 0 being the best score. Bangladesh, India and Sri Lanka have been given the best rating in South Asia at 0.25 and Pakistan and Bhutan the worst score at 0.75, with Nepal falling in between with scores of 0.50 (World Economic Forum, 2013).

Health services

Data on access of males and females at age one to DTP-3 to immunisation was available for five South Asian countries, namely Bangladesh, India, Maldives, Nepal and Pakistan. Shockingly, gender-disparities in access to DTP 3 immunisation exist in India, Nepal and Pakistan as of 2005-11, all in the direction of disadvantaging females . See Table 5 (WHO, 2013). This also points to the need for increasing community health workers, and insisting on state responsibility for ensuring universal immunisation coverage.

---

[13] The definition of 'forms of domestic violence' is not specified in the Global Gender Gap Report, 2013 (World Economic Forum, 2013).

Moving to reproductive health services, there is an unmet need for contraception of 12% globally as of 2005-12 (WHO, 2013). Data on unmet need for contraception for the same period was available for seven out of eight South Asian countries (other than Afghanistan). It indicates that unmet need is higher than global average in the case of four countries: Maldives, Nepal, Pakistan and India. See Table 5 for details. The high unmet need for contraception is surprising as it does well in delivering most health services   Another concern in South Asia is that the responsibility for a adopting contraceptive method falls mainly on women, while decisions are taken by men and in-laws. In India and Nepal, many men resist vasectomy due to myths that the procedure causes physical weakness or impotence (Family Health International, 2012)

Globally, 55% of pregnant women accessed four ANC visits- which is the global standard- as of as of 2005-12 (WHO, 2013). In Afghanistan, Bangladesh, India, Nepal and Pakistan the proportion of pregnant women accessing four ANCs was less than 55%, with the figure being an abysmal 15% as of 2005-12 in the case of Afghanistan (See Table 5). Access of pregnant women to four ANC visits was highest in Sri Lanka, though no separate data on access of ethnic minorities in the country was available.   There is no data on any South Asian country on proportion of pregnant women with HIV receiving ART. Globally, 57% of pregnant women with HIV receive ART, and this would be a useful data to get for each country in the region.

World over, 70% of pregnant women delivered under the hands of skilled health personnel as of 2005-11. In Sri-Lanka and Maldives the comparative figure was 93% and 85% suggested attention by the government to this aspect. In the other South Asian countries, the proportion of pregnant women who delivered under skilled health personnel ranged from 31% in the case of Bangladesh to 58% in the case of India and Bhutan as of 2005-11. See Table 5 for country wise data

Globally births by caesarean section are 16% as of 2005-11, which almost matches the upper end of the standard of '10-15% of births by Caesarean section' recommended by the World Health Organisation (Chaillet, 2007). However, in Sri Lanka, Maldives and Bangladesh this percentage is greater than the upper end of 10-15% recommended by WHO (in the first two countries by a greater margin) indicating possible misuse of caesarean sections for profit or misplaced preferences by women. On the other hand, the low proportion of births by caesarean section in Afghanistan and Nepal (5% and below) may indicate inadequate Comprehensive Emergency Obstetric care Globally 49% of women receive post-natal care (PNC) within two days of child birth as 2005-11. Only in Bhutan, Maldives and Sri Lanka did over 49% of women who had delivered receive post natal care within two days. See Table 5 for greater details.

Table 5: Access to health services

Country	DTP-3 immuni-sation by sex (one yr old)		Unmet need for FP	ANC four visits	Births attended by skilled personnel	Births by Caesarian section	PNC within two days of childbirth
Year	2005-11 M	F	2005-12	2005-12	2005-2011	2005-2011	2005-2011
Afghanistan	nd	nd	ND[14]	15	36	4	23
Bangladesh	91	91	12	26	31	17	27
Bhutan	nd	nd	12	77	58	12	66
India	58	53	21	50	58	8	48
Maldives	98	98	29	85	95	32	67
Nepal	92	91	27	50	36	5	45
Pakistan	62	55	25	28	45	7	39
Sri Lanka	nd	nd	7	93	99	24	71
Global	nd	nd	12	55	70	16	49

Source: WHO, 2013

Most maternal health services are better in urban than rural areas. Globally, they are more accessed by the women from top 20% than the bottom 20% of wealth quintile. Further, they are more utilized by those women with secondary education than those who are not literate (WHO, 2013). This is true for South Asia as well (ibid, 2013). While data for South Asia is not disaggregated by religion, caste, ethnicity or abilities, access to maternal health services is likely to lower amongst women from minority, Dalits, tribal and differently abled backgrounds.

---

[14] Contraceptive prevalence rate was 22% for the period 2005-2012

3.6 Health outcomes and demography

Data on health outcomes and few demographic indicators is given in Table 6. While life expectancy of females is greater than males in all the country there are concerns with regard to their health

According to Barot (2012) under normal circumstances sex ratio at birth ranges from 102–106 live male births per 100 live female births. As per statistics on sex ratio at birth (2005-2010) provided by the United Nations Population Division, the sex-ratio at birth is above this ratio in three of the 8 South Asian countries: India, Pakistan and Nepal (See Table 6 for details). This reveals a systemic gender-discrimination in these countries. In India, the sex ratio at birth started declining after 1980, in Nepal and Pakistan after 1995 (United Nations Population Division, n.d). Gender-discrimination along with privatisation of health care has contributed to the decline in sex ratio at birth. In Pakistan, the sex ratio at birth was worse in 2000-2005 than in 2005-2010, and has improved since then. As mentioned earlier prenatal sex selection and sex selective abortion affects women's health and perpetuates violence against women.

Table 6: Demographic and health outcome indicators

Country	Life expectancy at birth M F		Sex Ratio at birth	Children aged < 5 years who are stunted a (%)		Under-five mortality rate by sex[15]		MMR	Still Birth Rate[16]
Year	2011	2011	2005-10	2005-11 M	F	2005-11 M	F	2010	2009
Afghanistan	59	61	1.06	nd	nd	nd	nd	460	29
Bangladesh	69	70	1.05	44	42	75	71	240	36
Bhutan	66	69	1.04	nd	nd	nd	nd	180	22
India	64	67	1.11	48	48	82	88	200	22
Maldives	76	78	1.06	19	16	29	25	60	13
Nepal	67	69	1.07	41	39	62	62	170	23
Pakistan	66	68	1.09	nd	nd	93	93	260	47
Sri Lanka	71	78	1.04	nd	nd	nd	nd	35	17
Global	68	72	Nd	nd	nd	nd	nd	230	19

Source: WHO, 2013, UN Population Division, n.d

---

[15] Probability of dying by age 5 per 1000 live births.

[16] Per 1000 live births.

Sex-disaggregated data available from the World Health Statistics on percentage of children under five years who are stunted for four South Asian countries shows a male disadvantage in three countries: Bangladesh, Maldives and Nepal (See Table 6). This is not surprising as girls have greater biological resilience at birth. However, data for India shows no such female advantage, probably due to gender discrimination in access to immunisation and food/nutrition in India (see Table 5). Sex disaggregated data on under- five mortality was available for five countries, and points to higher male under five mortality in Bangladesh and Maldives, higher female under five mortality in India and same under five mortality rates in Nepal and Pakistan (See Table 6). Differences in immunisation and nutrition, along with differential access to health care lead to female disadvantage in under-five mortality rate in India.

Total fertility rate as of 2011 ranges from 1.7 in Maldives to 6.2 in Afghanistan, with the total fertility rate being above the global average of 2.4 in four out of the eight south Asian countries, namely India, Nepal, Pakistan and Afghanistan (See Table 6). The high total fertility rate in Afghanistan and Nepal is of particular concern as repeated pregnancies have a bearing on women's health and empowerment. Poor contraceptive services, poor reproductive rights or poverty could be reasons. A concern is the high adolescent fertility rate (higher than global average of 49) in Afghanistan, Bhutan and Nepal. Data in this regard was not available for Bangladesh (see Table 8). Adolescent fertility has a bearing on their health, as well as well-being and development and in South Asia is connected with early marriage of girls and lack of contraceptive services for adolescents (in particular unmarried adolescents).

Maternal mortality ratio in South Asia ranges from a low 35 in Sri Lanka (data on MMR across different ethnic groups not available) to a high 460 in Afghanistan in 2010 (See Table 6). Though MMR has declined in most South Asian countries, it is above the global average of 230 in three countries, namely Afghanistan, Bangladesh and Pakistan. Women's poor nutritional and social/economic status, unequal decision making power, inadequate access to contraception, inadequate transport facilities and inadequate access to comprehensive emergency obstetric health care services are problems. Unmet need for contraception is higher than the global average of 12% in four of seven South Asian countries on which data was available: India, Nepal, Maldives and Pakistan (no data for Afghanistan). This leads to unwanted pregnancies and unsafe abortions. Legal abortion is not in practice easily available in public facilities even in Nepal which has the most liberal abortion laws in South Asia (CEDAW, 2011a). High total fertility rates in four countries and adolescent fertility rates in three countries is another reasons for high rates of maternal mortality.

Reflecting maternal health and health services, is the still birth rate. Still birth rate as of 2009 is above the global average of 19 deaths per 1000 live birth in all the south Asian countries other than Sri Lanka and Maldives- two countries were per capita health expenditure per annum is comparatively higher. Still birth rate is highest in Afghanistan and lowest in Maldives.

4.0 Incorporation of Concluding Observations on health in latest national development plans.

The Concluding Observations of the Committee on Elimination of All Forms of Discrimination against Women (CEDAW) were available for all the South Asian countries other than Afghanistan (UN, n.de).

In this section a comparison is made between the Concluding Observations pertaining to health and the proposals in the health section of the latest national development plan of South Asian Countries (other than Afghanistan). An attempt is also made to review how far the insights emerging from the analysis of data of the preceding section is reflected in the health section of national development plans (for all .

4.1 Afghanistan

The goal of the health chapter of the Afghanistan National Development Strategy (2008-2013) is to improve the health and nutrition of the people of Afghanistan through quality health care service provision and promotion of healthy life-styles (Islamic Republic of Afghanistan, 2008). That is, the goal is not framed in a gender specific manner. Concretely it spells out that the government will reduce the MMR by 50% between 2002 and 2015 and to 25% of the 2002 level by 2020[17]. There are no targets on health indicators across life cycle of women

---

[17] Its targets on HIV, TB and malaria are not sex-disaggregated (Islamic Republic of Afghanistan, 2008).

Moving to the analysis of the context within the Health and Nutrition chapter of the National Development Plan, it notes that the percentage of health facilities with a woman doctor or nurse had increased from 26% in 2004 to 81% in 2007. It also notes that antenatal care (32% in 2006) and skilled birth attendance (19% in 2006) had improved, and so had contraceptive prevalence rate (16% in 2006). However it observes that MMR is high in Afghanistan. It notes gender-specific constraints like lack of female qualified health workers in rural areas. This context analysis could have benefitted out of analysis the fact that while maternal health services had improved in Afghanistan it was below the South Asian average (see Table 3). There is no mention of the restrictive abortion laws in the country, under which a woman undergoing abortion is punishable under Article 402 of the Penal Code. Further indoor pollution is high in Afghanistan with reliance on solid fuels. The implications of this are not analysed, (see Table 4). Gender gaps, disadvantaging women, with regard to elevated blood sugar levels while fasting and raised blood pressure, in contrast to the global trend, could have been highlighted in the Health and Nutrition Chapter (see Table 4). Lastly the implications for women of the fact that public expenditure on health as a percentage of total health expenditure is less than 25% could have been highlighted and its implications for poor women analysed (see Table 2)

Looking into the future, the Health and Nutrition chapter of the National Development Plan emphasises that it would further reproductive health and maternal and child health through providing ANC, skilled birth attendance, emergency obstetric care, post-natal care and family planning services. It commits to raising awareness on gender, health and rights, and increasing women's decision making on health. It further pledges to raise awareness on improving drinking water and sanitation. Interestingly, it commits to working with men on substance use and smoking, which is closely linked to violence against women and women's health respectively (through secondary smoking). It is not clear how the government of Afghanistan proposes to meet the WHO standard that countries should have at-least 23 health-care professionals (counting only physicians, nurses and midwives) per 10 000 population; in particular female physicians (Table 3). One could also add gynaecologists and psychiatrists (Islamic Republic of Afghanistan, 2008). Further, the fact that per capita investment in health needs to be increased to meet the standard of $ 53 per capita expenditure per annum is not mentioned (Table 2).

4.2 Bangladesh

The Bangladesh's Sixth Five Year Plan's (2011-2015) chapter on Health, Population and Nutrition Sector Development Programs aims to achieve improvement in the health, nutrition, and reproductive health (including family planning), particularly of vulnerable groups, including women, children, the elderly, and the poor (Planning Commission, 2011) The goal of the chapter is gender-specific, but does not use the language of non-discrimination or rights. Specific targets are set for reducing malnutrition, infant mortality and child mortality which laudably call for reducing gender disparities in these. Targets are also set for increasing proportion of pregnant women who access ante-natal care, delivery under skilled personnel and post natal care. Targets are also set for reducing anaemia amongst pregnant women and MMR. Making available reproductive health services for all is another (ambitious) target (Planning Commission, 2011).

The challenges that the government of Bangladesh identifies is poor maternal nutrition, access to caesarian for complications, early marriage and adolescent reproductive health, unmet need for family planning, violence against women and girls (including of differently abled), gender inequalities in accessing health care, reaching ethnic minorities and vulnerable areas, and low privacy in health facilities. Low per capita health expenditure, and public to total health expenditure is seen as a constraint to health of the population, including women. Looking into the future, the government proposes to evaluate its maternal voucher scheme and violence management strategy (within the health system), strengthen reproductive health services, address nutrition of women and girls (including maternal), prevent HIV/AIDS amongst women, make services women friendly train teachers and media on gender, health and disability. Interestingly it mentions that all sector facilities will treat 30% of patients (from low income groups, no mention of women) free of cost (Planning Commission, 2011).

The analysis and committed strategies under the Sixth Five year Plan are partly in keeping with Concluding Observations of the CEDAW of March 2011 on the reports submitted by the government of Bangladesh, which are summarized in Table 7. This speaks of perhaps the involvement of women's health movement in in the government planning process. Some additional concerns (to what is reflected in the Sixth Five Year Plan) expressed by the Concluding Observations from the CEDAW are the lack of disaggregated data on women's health in the state report to CEDAW. It draws attention to the fact that while MMR has declined, it is still high. The Concluding Comment additionally draws attention to poor health of women headed households, Dalit women, migrant women, refugee women, older women, and girls living on the streets. Finally, it highlights the poor quality of health services for women, in particular in rural areas. Looking into the future, it highlights a few additional strategies to what is outlined in the Sixth Five Year Plan, like raising awareness on contraception, risks of unsafe abortion and reproductive rights, providing safe and affordable contraception and strengthening collection of sex disaggregated data on health. Concluding Observations on other Articles mentions the need to train health personnel on providing support to victims of violence against women (CEDAW, 2011b). See Table 7 for details on the Concluding Observations made by CEDAW in 2011 on Bangladesh.

Table 7: CEDAW (2011) Concluding Observations: Bangladesh

Positive developments	Concerns	Recommendations
Establishment of women friendly model district hospitals Establishment of women friendly Upazilla (sub-district) health complexes	On Article 12 Lack of disaggregated data on women's health situation in the State party's report to CEDAW Inadequate attention to women's reproductive health-care services. Despite decline, maternal mortality remains high Women's inadequate access to quality health care services, including reproductive health services- in particular in rural areas On Other Articles Unequal access of rural women headed households, Dalit women, migrant women, refugee women, older women, women with disabilities and girls living on the streets to quality health services	On Article 12 Improve women's access to quality health-care facilities and services including those related to reproductive health care, with special attention to disadvantaged women Adequate pre- and postnatal care and access to trained birth attendants Raise awareness on contraception, risks of unsafe abortion and women's reproductive rights Ensure access to safe and affordable contraception On Other Articles Collect data on health status of women, including disaggregated data across disadvantaged groups and improve their situation Train health personnel on providing gender-sensitive support for survivors of VAW

Source: CEDAW, 2011b

If one compares the section on Health, Population and Nutrition Sector Development Programs within the Sixth Five Year Plan and the analysis of health data on Bangladesh (Section 3). it is apparent that the section well takes into account the issues emerging from the sex-disaggregated statistics. The Plan could have paid more attention gendered health risks like poor access to sanitation and safe cooking fuel (Table 4). Similarly, attention could have been given to higher risk of women than men in Bangladesh to raised glucose levels while fasting and to raised blood pressure (Table 3). Abortion laws in the country are restrictive, with abortion being permitted to save lives of the pregnant women. It is not clear how the government of Bangladesh proposes to meet the WHO standard that countries should have at-least 23 health-care professionals (counting only physicians, nurses and midwives) per 10 000 population. (Table 3). Further, the fact that per capita investment in health needs to be increased to meet the standard of $ 53 per capita expenditure per annum is not mentioned in the section on Health, Population and Nutrition.

4.3 Bhutan

The goal of sub-section on health within the Bhutan Eleventh Five Year Plan (2013-2018) is to deliver quality medical services and increase access of all citizens of the country to health care (Royal Government of Bhutan, 2013). It does not specifically mention women as citizens or access of women sex/gender-specific health services like maternal health services. Nevertheless, its targets include reduction of MMR, increased access of pregnant women to Prevention of Parent to Child Transmission (of HIV/AIDS) services and increase in contraceptive prevalence rate. Interestingly, the health chapter spells out targets on improved sanitation as well reducing alcohol and tobacco use (not specified amongst women or men). As mentioned, reducing alcohol consumption by men is known to reduce domestic violence against women, and reducing tobacco use by men reduces secondary infection of lungs by women. The government recognises that it has made progress towards health targets outlined in MDGS, but notes that non-communicable diseases are increasing (Royal Government of Bhutan, 2013). Due to demographic changes, adolescent and older people's health are emerging as new issues. As Bhutan is prone to disasters (landslides), health services in disasters are concerns. The section on health observes that migratory and peri-urban communities are lagging behind in health indicators. Its proposed strategies include strengthening nutrition services with a focus on the girl child, adolescent health services, RCH services (including maternal health and contraception), prevention & management of sexually transmitted infections (including HIV/AIDS), mental health services, management of cases of violence against women, and alcohol and tobacco use (especially amongst men) (Royal Government of Bhutan, 2013).

Table 8: CEDAW (2009) Concluding Observations: Bhutan

Positive developments	Concerns	Recommendations
Free access to traditional and modern health care; resource commitment	Lack of disaggregated statistics on health of women; including on breast, uterine and ovarian cancer	Continue to improve women's access to general, mental health and reproductive health, including of older women, and women in rural and remote areas.
Progress in certain areas of maternal and reproductive health care	Lack of data regarding the frequency of medical consultations for pregnant women

Lack of information on | Report on an integral health policy for women, covering cancer screening |

Progress on access to contraception	family planning measures and sex education for young and adolescent girls; impact on teenage pregnancy	Increase women's access to health-care and confidential medical assistance by trained personnel, in particular in rural and remote areas
	Prevalence of HIV/AIDS amongst women under the age of 25	Promote family planning and reproductive health amongst girls and boys, with special attention to prevention of early pregnancies and the control of STIs
	Limited access to confidential care	To carry out research to determine the factors leading to the feminization of HIV/AIDS, and develop strategies.

Source: CEDAW, 2009

The analysis and committed strategies under the Eleventh Five year Plan is partly in keeping with Concluding Observations of the CEDAW (CEDAW, 2009). The Concluding Observations pertaining to Bhutan additionally highlight the need for statistics in particular on breast, uterine and ovarian cancer, frequency of medical consultations by pregnant women, teenage pregnancies, and prevalence of HIV/AIDS amongst women less than 25 years. Lack of privacy in health facilities is an additional issue highlighted in the Concluding Observations, Bhutan. The Concluding Observations urge the government of Bhutan to evolve a Women's Health Policy covering reproductive cancers, ensure women's confidential access to health services, prevention of early pregnancies and STIs amongst young women and to carry out research on the reason for the feminisation of HIV/AIDS in the country. It places particular emphasis on ensuring health of rural women and women in remote areas (CEDAW, 2009). See Table 8 for details on the Concluding Observations made by CEDAW in 2009 on Bhutan

The health component of the Eleventh Five Year Plan of Bhutan (2013-2018) well takes into account what the sex disaggregated statistics analysed in Section 3 reveal on women's health in Bhutan. A few exceptions are that the Plan does not take into account loopholes with regard to gender and health legislation. Abortion is legally available for specific reasons like saving the life of the women, to preserve mental health and in instances of rape and incest; and not on demand. Legislation on domestic- violence are considered weak in Bhutan and the implications of domestic violence for women's health/health services are not analysed. The gender-intensified health risks faced by Bhutanese women highlighted in Section 3 like poor access to safe cooking fuel, fairly high adolescent fertility rate, raised glucose levels while fasting (higher than men). Sex disaggregated data on prevalence of alcohol and tobacco use amongst those less than 25 years and use of condom during high risk sex is not available for Bhutan, making diagnosis and planning difficult. This data gap could have been bridged in the Eleventh Plan. It is not clear how the government of Bhutan proposes to meet the WHO standard that countries should have at-least 23 health-care professionals (counting only physicians, nurses and midwives) per 10 000 population. The number of health care professionals in Bhutan is far lower than this global standard. Further, the fact that per capita investment in health needs to be increased to meet the standard of $ 53 per capita expenditure per annum is not mentioned.

4.4 India

Interestingly the Chapter on Health within the 12th Five Year Plan (2012-2017) of the Indian government does not outline a specific goal or objective, but includes targets such as reduction in MMR, anaemia amongst women in reproductive age and total fertility rate (Planning Commission, 2013). It notes that the government has improved institutional delivery through cash incentives to pregnant women. However, it observes that challenges remain with regard to women's health. The chapter notes that availability public health-service is poor, and quality and affordability are issues in the private health sector. The Health Chapter discerns that the burden of non-communicable diseases is increasing. It further highlights that child sex ratio has worsened in the country, and 11th Plan targets have not been met with regard to MMR, ante-natal care, skilled birth attendance and total fertility rate. It reflects that anaemia and malnutrition amongst women are high, as well as unmet need for contraception. Early marriage persists.

The strategies proposed by the Indian government include provision of universal health care services through public health facilities. Concretely the governments plans to provide iron and folic acid for pregnant women and adolescent girls, deworming of women of reproductive age, access to contraception and safe abortion services, prevention of parent to child transmission of HIV/AIDS free of cost, education on SRH to adolescents, screening of cervical & breast cancer, prevention of tobacco use amongst men. It also mentions making health facilities accessible and relevant to disabled, Dalits, Adivasis, elderly, minorities, and migrants. On the institutional side, the 12th Five year Plan commits to decentralised health planning and monitoring, and collection of sex disaggregated data on disease burden and access to treatment (Planning Commission, 2013).

The Concluding Observations of the CEDAW on India, November 2010 does not include a separate section on health, and is hence brief on this issue (CEDAW, 2010). Its observations appear only to be partly taken into account in the section on Health within the 12th Five Year Plan of India (2012-2017). The Concluding Observations note the poor access of women and girls in displaced camps post Gujarat riots to basic needs including water, sanitation and health/reproductive health care services (see Table 9).. The issue of health services for women in conflict and other emergencies is not well addressed in the 12th Five Year Plan. The other recommendation of the CEDAW is to train health personnel on providing gender-sensitive support for survivors of violence against women. This is not mentioned in the Health Chapter of 12th Five Year Plan, though the Chapter on Women's Agency and Child Rights notes growing violence against women. This chapter also emphasises the need to provide health services to transgender persons (Planning Commission, 2013). The lack of attention to strengthen health service provision to survivors of violence against women and transgender people within the health chapter is a concern

Table 9: CEDAW (2010) Concluding Observations: India

Positive developments	Concerns related to health	Recommendations
No comments	Poor access of women and girls in displaced camps post Gujarat riots to food, water, sanitation, shelter and health care-including reproductive health services	Strengthen access of women and girls in internally displaced camps to food, water, sanitation, shelter and health care-including reproductive health services Train health personnel on providing gender-sensitive support for survivors of VAW

Source: CEDAW, 2010

The chapter on Health of the Twelfth Five Year Plan (2012-2017) of India partially addressed issues raised by the health statistics and laws on India. The Plan includes strategies to strengthen sanitation, antenatal care, skilled birth attendance, contraception and reduce smoking and tobacco use amongst men. However, it does not take into state its plan for rectifying the fact that government expenditure on health to total health expenditure is only 28% or that majority of private expenditure comes from out of pocket health expenditure burdening poor and marginalised women. Strategies to address skewed sex ratio at birth and bridge gender differentials in immunization at age 1 and under five mortality rate (Table 5) would be useful. While improving antenatal and skilled birth attendance are targets, there is none around improving access to post natal care, which is low for India. There is no attention paid in the 12th Five Year Plan (or Concluding Observations) on the poor access to safe fuels for cooking. Lack of adequate knowledge on HIV/AIDS amongst young women and gender gaps in knowledge is yet another concern, as well as poor (and lower) ability of women to negotiate condom in high risk sex (Table 4).

4.5 Maldives
The objective of the sub-section on Quality and Affordable Health Care for all within the National Framework for Development (2009-2013) of Maldives is to provide affordable basic healthcare as a fundamental human right and an integral component of socio-economic development. While the objectives are not gender-specific, the sub-section (elsewhere) mentions that the government will protect the health rights of women, children, elderly and disabled (Government of Maldives, 2009).

While observing that Maldives is on target with regard to MDGs on Maternal and Child Health, the government notes with concern the existence of malnutrition and micro nutrient deficiency amongst women of reproductive age, the inadequate access to safe drinking water and improved sanitation, increase in non-communicable diseases, expatriate work force who are unable to communicate with the local community, and inadequate services in atoll[18] population. The Framework for Development of Maldives mentions that it will strengthen services in the area of safe motherhood and reproductive health, provision of reproductive health commodities, diagnosis and treatment of cancers, treatment for violence against women and provide age and sex appropriate adolescent sexual reproductive health education. It also emphasizes that it will strengthen programs to prevent and address mental health and disability, as well as HIV/AIDS. The Framework for Development commits itself to a universal health insurance (Government of Maldives 2009)

---

[18] An **atoll** is a ring-shaped **coral reef**, island, or series of islets (National Geographic, n.d).

The Plan integrates some of CEDAW's 2007 Concluding Observations pertaining to health but not all (CEDAW, 2007, See Table 10). While applauding the RH strategy on Women, Men and Adolescents, the CEDAW notes several areas of discrimination and concern with regard to women's health. It observes the poor status of women in atoll areas which makes it difficult for them to access health services. It notes that law limits contraception to married couples, and that women have little choice over spacing and choice of contraceptive methods. Sexual rights of women are not respected by the Penal Code with punishments such as flogging and banishment if women are found having extra-marital relationships. At the same time, the Observations, note, there is a high rate of polygamy and early marriage in the country which goes unpunished. The additional strategies suggested in the Concluding Observations, which are not reflected in the National Development Framework, are strengthening access of women to sexual health services, revision of Penal Code to ensure that extra martial affairs are not punishable and revision of Family Law so that it is consistent with Article 16 of the Convention.

Table 10: CEDAW (2007) Concluding Observations: Maldives

Positive developments	Concerns related to health	Recommendations
Action plan to implement the recommendations of the "Study on Women, Health and Life Experience" conducted by the Ministry of Gender and Family Presence of a reproductive health strategy for women, men and adolescents	Poor status of women's health, particularly of women in the rural (atolls) areas, who experience difficulties in accessing specialized health services in a timely manner Limited control that women have over the choice of family planning methods and spacing of children Law limits contraception to married couples Punishments such as flogging and banishment remain in the Penal Code and are imposed on women suspected for extramarital sex High rate of early marriage and polygamy	Integrate a gender perspective into health sector reforms so that women in the atolls have equal access to services. Ensure women's access to health services including SRH services in accordance with the Convention Make comprehensive range of contraceptive services available, including information, education & communication Integrate age appropriate sex education into curriculum, with special focus on STIs and unwanted pregnancy Revise Penal Code so that extra marital affairs are not punishable Fix a time frame to revise family law so that it is in keeping with Article 16 of the Convention Train health personnel on providing gender-sensitive support for survivors of violence against women

Source: CEDAW, 2007

The health component of the National Development Framework partially concerns raised by the health statistics on Maldives. In the context of the fact that private health expenditure as a percentage of total health expenditure is 39%, the Framework's proposal to promote universal health insurance is extremely important for both poor women and men. Its emphasis on addressing unmet need for contraception is also crucial. However, there is no analysis of, or commitment to change, the high proportion of births by caesarean sections at 24% which is higher than the global norm of 10-15% (Table 5). Removing restrictions on abortions- which is only available for saving the lives of the pregnant women or preserve her physical health-is not mentioned, as well as making safe abortions available. The proportion of men who use tobacco is high at 43%[19] and this is likely to have secondary impact on women's health which is not analysed in the Framework (See Table 4).

4.6 Nepal

The sub-section on Population, Health and Nutrition within the Approach Paper[20] to the 13th Plan (2013-2015) of the government of Nepal outlines three objectives of which one is to establish reproductive rights as fundamental human rights (National Planning Commission, 2013). While noting that the maternal mortality ratio has reduced in Nepal due to free delivery, the sub section on health observes that health situation of Dalits, Madhesis, Muslims, disabled, endangered ethnic groups, residents of remote hills and mountainous regions is lagging behind, in particular that of women. It makes a commitment to strengthen access of these groups to health services. The sub-section also commits to improving

[19] The comparative figure for women is 11%.
[20] The final draft document was not available at the time of drafting this paper.

awareness and services related to family planning, maternal health services, safe-abortion services and reproductive health, and interestingly improve men's participation in population stabilisation. The Approach Paper mentions that it will set up nutritional rehabilitation centers for pregnant women. Other areas that are prioritized are raising awareness and counseling on sexual and reproductive health and HIV/AIDS, as well as harmful effects of alcoholism, smoking and substance use. It proposes to roll preventive and curative services related to mental health, and establish health protocols and capacities to address cases of violence against women (National Planning Commission, 2013).

The analysis and recommendations of the sub-section on health of the Approach Paper, 13th Plan is partially in keeping with the Concluding Observations on Nepal. See Table 11 below. The Concluding Observations, in addition to the concerns raised in the Approach Paper, highlights the need for strengthening access of rural, poor and young mothers to emergency obstetric care, of women who had been subject to sexual violence in conflict settings to appropriate health and support services, and of adolescents to family planning services. It highlights the high prevalence of uterine prolapse, and the need for services to address these problems. It also calls for addressing harmful practices like chapuadi[21] and gender discrimination in food. On the institutional front, the Concluding Observation call for more female doctors and sex-disaggregated health statistics (See Table 11)

---

[21] The tradition under which women/adolescent girls are forced to sleep in sheds or outbuildings during their monthly periods. Adolescent girls have to skip schools (The Guardian, 2014)

Table 11: CEDAW (2007) Concluding Observations: Nepal

Positive developments	Concerns related to health	Recommendations
Scheme for free delivery services and the decrease in the maternal mortality ratio	Substantive gender equality lacking in health; in particular for women facing multiple forms of discrimination. Poor access to health care by poor, rural and differently abled women (including contraception) Persistence of high MMR and morbidity amongst rural, poor and young mothers; challenge in accessing emergency obstetric care Poor nutrition of women, correlated with maternal morbidity and mortality High prevalence of uterine prolapse and unsafe abortion for marginalized women Lack of data on HIV prevalence among pregnant women Mental and physical health needs of survivors of sexual violence during conflict	Strengthen antenatal, postnatal and emergency obstetric care services, in particular for poor women, rural women and young mothers; Address harmful practices against women and girls which affect women's health like Chaupadi and gender discrimination in food Take measures to prevent uterine prolapse including access to contraception, funds for corrective surgeries, and follow up visits Improve access to abortion services Universal access to the full range of contraceptive methods including emergency contraception Enforce legal age of marriage of 20 years Train health care providers on addressing/treating domestic and sexual violence against women, while also raising awareness on this issue at the community level (including with men and boys) Establish counseling and health services for survivors of sexual violence during conflict, and engender Truth

			and Reconciliation Commissions
			Increase number of medical staff, including female doctors for rural women, poor women and women with disabilities

Source: CEDAW, 2007a

The health component of the Approach Paper partially addresses gender and health issues raised through the health statistics on Maldives presented in Section 3. It seeks to address the high MMR, low access to ante-natal care, low proportion of births attended by skilled attendance and low access to post-natal care. It however does not commit to increasing government health expenditure on health (including social health insurance). The Approach Paper does not have a strategy to comprehensive strategy to address skewed sex ratio at birth or high adolescent fertility rate at 81 (Table 6). Moving to risks to women's health, the Approach Paper does not recognise or spell out strategies to address the inadequate sanitation and unhealthy cooking fuel situation in the country. The fact that 36% of men and 29% of women smoke poses indirect and direct health risks to women is also not mentioned in the Approach Paper (see Table 4). In Nepal, more proportion of women record elevated blood pressure than men; the Approach paper does not have a strategy to address this (Table 4). Lastly, awareness of how HIV/AIDS is transmitted is inadequate amongst youth, in particular women.

While the importance of preventing smoking and improving knowledge on HIV are recognised in the Approach Paper, the gendered implications and gaps in information on not recognised. Lastly, It is a concern that data is not available on number of community health workers, nurses and midwives and physicians per 10000 population is not available (National Planning Commission, 2013). Further, the fact that per capita investment in health needs to be increased to meet the standard of $ 53 per capita expenditure per annum is not mentioned.

4.7 Pakistan

The objective of the sub sections on 'Healthy Population" and 'Population Challenge" within the Vision 2030 document is a healthy and productive population-across gender, social identity, income and residence (Planning Commission, 2007). Some of the concrete targets include strengthening access to improved water & sanitation and reducing maternal mortality and morbidity. The sub-sections note that Pakistan lags behind on reproductive health related MDG targets. It observes that reducing fertility is important for health of women, as well as improving women's labour force participation rates and reducing budget allocation for women's health in the long run. The sections perceive that while women outlive men, chronic diseases are more likely to affect women.

The sub-sections propose integration of various female health cadres so as to ensure universal coverage of reproductive health services (including contraception) along with referral services for complicated deliveries. Lady Health Workers, it is envisaged, will also promote community health insurance and micro finance. Any shortage of nurses would be addressed through private sector involvement. Nutritional supplementation of women is another is another priority. Interestingly the government proposes constitution of an inter-sectoral health board with links to civil society. It is not clear whether the Department related to women's development would be involved in the Board (Planning Commission, 2007).

The sections on 'Healthy Population" and 'Population Challenge" within Vision 2030 partially takes into account the Concluding Observations on health of the CEDAW Committee of June 2007 (CEDAW, 2007b). The Concluding Observations devote two paragraphs to health. While applauding the progress in women's health where Lady Health Workers have been posted it is concerned about the lack of sexual health services, high incidence of unsafe abortions linked to poor contraceptive services, and the link between unsafe abortion and high maternal mortality (See Table 12). These are issues not touched by the two sections. In addition to strategies proposed under 'Healthy Population" and 'Population Challenge" of the Vision 2030, the Concluding Observations call for strengthening sexual health services particularly in rural areas, increasing awareness amongst men on contraception, reviewing the laws punishing women who undergo abortion, providing safe abortion services and training health service providers so that they can respond to violence against women (CEDAW, 2007b)

Table 12: CEDAW (2007) Concluding Observations: Pakistan

Positive developments	Concerns related to health	Recommendations
Improvement in the indicators of women's health where the Lady Health Worker programme is being implemented	Women's lack of access to health care, in particular to sexual and reproductive health services, especially in rural areas The adverse effect of low contraceptive use on unsafe abortion. Clandestine abortions are a major cause of maternal mortality	Take concrete measures to enhance women's access to health care, in particular to sexual and reproductive health services and in rural areas To ensure comprehensive range of contraceptives are available widely and affordably, without any restrictions, and increase awareness about family planning among women and men. Reduce maternal mortality by addressing causes of maternal death. Review the laws relating to abortion, remove punishment of women who undergo abortion, and provide women with access to quality services for the management of complications arising from unsafe abortion Expand the Lady Health Worker Programme to rural and other areas Train health service providers to ensure they can respond to violence against women

Source: CEDAW, 2007b

The health component of the Vision 2030 document partially addresses gender and health issues raised in the WHO health statistics on Pakistan (Section 3).   It seeks to tackle poor maternal nutrition (reflected in high rates of still births), inadequate access to maternal health care services, high total fertility rate and maternal mortality ratio (Tables 5 and 6). However it is not clear how maternal mortality ratio can be lowered with reforming the laws on abortion and strengthening provision of safe abortion services. However, skewed sex ratio at birth, gender differences in access to immunisation of one year old, high rates of caesarean sections, and elevated blood sugar while fasting (more than men) are not mentioned in the Health section of the Vision 2030 document. Health hazards of using sold fuels for cooking by women and of women being secondary smokers with one third of men smoking are not discussed. Total expenditure on health is minimal at $ PPP 10 per capita per, and the health chapter does not state how the per capita investment in health will eb increased to meet the standard of $ 53 per capita expenditure per annum. On the positive side, the government expenditure on health total health expenditure is high (77%) and this merits highlighting; and this merits highlighting in the Vision 2030 (Table 2)

4.8 Sri Lanka

The section on a 'Healthy Society' within Mahinda Chintana aims at creating a healthier nation that contributes to its economic, social, mental and spiritual development (Department of National Planning, 2010). Its targets include 100% ante-natal care coverage and skilled birth attendance, and reduction of maternal mortality ratio. The section considers the provision of free health and MCH services, and initiation of gender based violence programme as its strengths. Some of the challenge it points to are emergency of non-communicable diseases, persistent under nutrition amongst mothers (in-spite of food package programme) and unequal access of low income groups to health care. It proposes to strengthen nutrition amongst adolescents and pregnant women, launch a national HIV/AIDS programme, provide counseling and support/treatment to widows, elderly, disabled and those living with mental illness and addiction, It mentions that hospitals for cancers would be established though there is no specific reference to treatment of reproductive cancers (Department Of National Planning, 2010).

The section on a 'Healthy Society' is only partly in keeping with the Concluding Observations of April 2011 of the CEDAW (CEDAW, 2011c). While noting that Sri Lanka is on track on improving maternal health, it notes the low use of contraception, teenage pregnancies in conflict ridden areas, maternal deaths due to unsafe abortion, sexual violence in conflict ridden areas and the lack of water, sanitation & shelter facilities in these areas. These are issues not covered in the section on Healthy Society. The Concluding Observations call for strengthening sexual and reproductive health services for internally displaced women and girls (contraception and control of STIs and HIV/AIDS). Another recommendation is to strengthen water, sanitation and shelter facilities in these areas. The Concluding Observations further emphasize the need for removing punitive measures against women undergoing abortions, and providing quality abortion services and services to manage complications arising out of unsafe abortion (CEDAW, 2011c).   The Concluding Observations also call for sensitizing health personnel that violence against women is a criminal offense. See Table 13 for details.

The section on a 'Healthy Society' of the Mahinda Chintana partially addresses gender and health issues raised through the WHO health statistics on Sri Lanka (Section 3). A concern emerging from the statistics is that over the years private health expenditure as a percentage of total health expenditure has overshot public health expenditure (though not to the extent of Afghanistan and India). There are not any strategies outlined in the section on Healthy Society to combat this. There are no approaches to address the higher rates of caesarean sections (24%) than the WHO norm of 10-15%, or the adverse consequences of smoking amongst men on women (see Tables 4 and 5) . There is a need for sex disaggregated statistics on immunisation, stunting amongst under five, correct knowledge amongst youth on HIV/AIDS and use of condoms during high risk sex.   There is no data on number of community health workers per 10000 population. These health workers, normally women, play an important role in reaching women

Table 13: <u>CEDAW (2011) Concluding Observations: Sri Lanka</u>

Positive developments	Concerns related to health	Recommendations
On track in improving maternal health (MDG-5)	Limited knowledge of reproductive health Low access & use of contraceptives The high level of teenage pregnancies especially in conflict-affected areas The increase in prevalence of HIV/AIDS among women Abortion is punishable under law other than if mother's life is at threat, and 10% of maternal mortality is due to clandestine abortion Sexual violence allegedly perpetrated also by the armed forces, the police and militant groups. Inadequate water, health, sanitation and shelter facility in conflict areas.	Promote reproductive health education for internally displaced women and girls with a focus on contraception, control of STIs and HIV/AIDS and prevention of unwanted pregnancies Reduce unsafe abortion through removing punitive measures, providing quality abortion services, and managing complications arising out of abortions. Reduce maternal mortality by addressing root causes Provide health, water, sanitation and shelter facilities to internally displaced persons and returnees Sensitise health service providers that violence against women constitutes a criminal offence

Source: CEDAW, 2011c

5.0 Conclusion

This paper sought to examine how far the analysis and recommendations from Concluding Observations of the CEDAW on health are taken into account in the sections on health of the national development plans of seven South Asian countries (other than Afghanistan). It also sought to explore how far the sections of the national development plan on health reflect sex-disaggregated health statistics and information available on eight South Asian countries.

The review suggests that the health sections of most national development plans partially take into account the Concluding Observations of CEDAW. The gaps were larger in countries recovering from conflict. The gaps between Concluding Observations and national development plans on women's health were largest with regard to 'controversial' issues' like legalising abortion, providing safe abortion services, providing sexual health services and providing treatment to survivors of violence against women. Treatment for low priority issues like mental health, uterine prolapse and reproductive cancers were missed out by some national governments, while emphasised in Concluding Observations. The gaps between Concluding Comments and national development plans were higher with regard to health/sexual and reproductive health of 'controversial groups'; like internally displaced women and girls, unwed adolescent girls and women, and women were married but in other relationships. Yet another gap was between the repeated call for sex-disaggregated health statistics in Concluding Observations and the limited attention to these in health sub sections of national development plans. The Concluding Observations noted the links between social determinants of health like access to improved water and , sanitation, but this did not always receive attention in the national development plans.

A comparison between data and information on gender disparities in health and health legislation   and the health sections of the national development plans suggest that the interconnection between health financing and women's health is not made. This is a concern in five out of eight South Asian countries, wherein the proportion of private health expenditure to total health is more than public; which implies that poor women more than men would not be able to access health services and may become more indebted. Unnecessary caesarean sections are higher in private sector. Further per capita health expenditure is below US 53 PPP in five South Asian countries, which is extremely low.   Similarly the analysis of interconnections between health systems and women's health is insufficient. In particular, the fact that the sum total of health workers, physicians and nurses is below the WHO norms in 75% of South Asian countries is not recognised. While depression is higher amongst women than men in South Asia like elsewhere, the number of psychiatrist per 10000 population is below 0.05 in all but one South Asian country.   Though data from three out of five South Asian countries (on which data was available) shows gender disparities in access to immunisation it is not analysed in the national development plans. Sex ratio at birth is skewed in three South Asian countries, but receives attention in the health chapter of only one national development plan. The over reliance on female contraceptive methods by the government and couples is not addressed in the national development plans.   Data on elevated fasting glucose and elevated blood pressure indicates that in four and three South Asian countries there is a female disadvantage contrary to the global trend. This gender difference has not received emphasis in the national development plans.   While combatting alcoholism, smoking and other substance use is mentioned in several plans, there is no analysis of gender differences in use and sex/gender differentiated secondary impact.   Data available from one county suggests inadequate and lower knowledge on HIV amongst young women, as well as actual use of condoms at high risk sex. This is another aspect that needs looking into, including provision of female condoms through government facilities. It is data on maternal and child health and contraception that is used for planning in most South Asian countries, but not information on legal status of abortion or availability of safe abortion services (other than for sex-selection).

To sum up, the Concluding Observations and available data/information is only partially used in the health sections of the national development plans. To address this gap it is suggested that the CEDAW encourages South Asian governments to incorporate comments on each sector into their national planning process, and report back to the CEDAW as to how the Concluding Observations were incorporated. It is also suggested that the CEDAW and the national governments together identity gender and health experts (well versed with the Convention), public health financing experts, women' federations and women's health rights groups who could be part of the planning process of the health section of the national development plan. The Ministry of Women's Affairs in each country could also be involved in planning of health section of national development plans. The plans should incorporate not only the Concluding Observations pertaining to health, but also the principles enshrined in the General Recommendation on Health. The national governments and other stakeholders, while planning the health section, must identify and analyse sex-disaggregated data on health financing, health risks, health systems, health laws, health services and health outcomes. There is a danger that if such integration does not happen the Concluding Observations, global gender and health data and national development plans go in different directions.

Reference

Asian Legal Research Center, n.d, Glossary of terms used in international law relating to treaties and conventions, http://hrli.alrc.net/mainfile.php/glossary/130/

Barot, S, 2012, A Problem-and-Solution Mismatch: Son Preference and Sex-Selective Abortion Bans, Guttmacher Policy Review, Spring 2012, Volume 15, Number 2, http://www.guttmacher.org/pubs/gpr/15/2/gpr150218.html

Bahuguna, 2010, Elected Women Representatives from Grass-Root Communities of India – Improving Community Health and Ensuring Accountability, Poster Presentation at Geneva Health Forum, 2010, http://ghf.globalhealthforum.net/2012/11/12/elected-women-representatives-from-grass-root-communities-of-india-improving-community-health-and-ensuring-accountability/#.U4V4ovmSzLE

CEDAW, 1999, CEDAW General Recommendation No. 24: Article 12 of the Convention (Women and Health), 1999, A/54/38/Rev.1, chap. I, http://www.refworld.org/docid/453882a73.html

CEDAW, 2007a, Concluding Observations of the Committee on the Elimination of Discrimination against Women Maldives, Committee on the Elimination of Discrimination against Women, Thirty-seventh session 15 January-2 February 2007 http://daccess-dds-ny.un.org/doc/UNDOC/GEN/N07/243/86/PDF/N0724386.pdf?OpenElement

CEDAW, 2007b, Concluding Observations of the Committee on the Elimination of Discrimination against Women Pakistan, Committee on the Elimination of Discrimination against Women, Thirty-eighth session, 14th May-1 June, 2007 http://daccess-dds-ny.un.org/doc/UNDOC/GEN/N07/376/08/PDF/N0737608.pdf?OpenElement

CEDAW, 2009, Concluding observations of the Committee on the Elimination of Discrimination against Women Bhutan, Committee on the Elimination of Discrimination against Women, Forty-fourth session 20 July-7 August 2009 http://www.iwraw-ap.org/committee/pdf/44_concluding_observations/bhutan.pdf

CEDAW, 2010, Concluding observations of the Committee on the Elimination of Discrimination against Women India, Committee on the Elimination of Discrimination against Women Forty-seventh session 4–22 October 2010, http://www.iwraw-ap.org/committee/pdf/47_concluding_observations/india.pdf

CEDAW, 2011a, Concluding observations of the Committee on the Elimination of Discrimination against Women Nepal, Committee on the Elimination of Discrimination against Women Forty-ninth session 11-29 July 2011, http://www2.ohchr.org/english/bodies/cedaw/docs/co/CEDAW-C-NPL-CO-4-5.pdf

CEDAW, 2011b, Concluding observations of the Committee on the Elimination of Discrimination against Women Nepal, Committee on the Elimination of Discrimination against Women Forty-eight Session, 17 January – 4 February 2011 http://www2.ohchr.org/english/bodies/cedaw/docs/co/CEDAW-C-NPL-CO-4-5.pdf

CEDAW, 2011c, Concluding observations of the Committee on the Elimination of Discrimination against Women Nepal, Committee on the Elimination of Discrimination against Women, Forty-eighth session
17 January – 4 February 2011
http://www2.ohchr.org/english/bodies/cedaw/docs/co/CEDAW-C-LKA-CO-7.pdf

Centre for Global Development, n.d, MDG Progress Index: Gauging Country-Level Achievements,
http://www.cgdev.org/page/mdg-progress-index-gauging-country-level-achievements

Chaillet, N, E, Dubé, M Dugas, D. Francoeur, J Dubé, S.Gagnon, L Poitras, A Dumont, 2007, Identifying barriers and facilitators towards implementing guidelines to reduce caesarean section rates in Quebec, Bulletin of the World Health Organization Volume 85, Number 10, October 2007, 733-82
http://www.who.int/bulletin/volumes/85/10/06-039289/en/

Christian P, KP West, J Katz, E Kimbrough-Pradhan, SC, LeClerq , SK Khatry, SR, Shrestha,2004, Cigarette smoking during pregnancy in rural Nepal. Risk factors and effects of beta-carotene and vitamin A supplementation. Eur J Clin Nutr. 2004 Feb;58(2):204-11.
http://www.nature.com/ejcn/journal/v58/n2/full/1601767a.html

Department Of National Planning, 2010, Sri Lanka The Emerging Wonder of Asia, Mahinda Chintana – Vision for the Future, The Development Policy Framework, Department Of National Planning, Ministry Of Finance And Planning, Democratic Socialist Republic of Sri Lanka, Colombo. www.treasury.gov.lk/.../mahindaChintanaVision-2010full-eng.pdf

Family Health International (FHI), 2012, Increasing Men's Engagement to Improve Family Planning Programs in South Asia, FHI, NC/USA and New Delhi/India. http://www.fhi360.org/sites/default/files/media/documents/MaleEngageBrief.pdf

Government of India, 1994, Pre-Conception & Pre-Natal Diagnostic Techniques Act, 1994, http://pndt.gov.in/writereaddata/mainlinkFile/File50.pdf

Government of Maldives, 2009, "Aneh Dhivehiraajje" - The Strategic Action Plan, National Development Framework for 2009 – 2013, The President's Office, Government of Maldives, Male. http://planning.gov.mv/en/images/stories/publications/strategic_action_plan/SAP-EN.pdf

Islamic Republic Of Afghanistan, N.D Afghanistan National Development Strategy (2008-13), An Interim Strategy For Security, Governance, Economic Growth & Poverty Reduction, Volume I, Government Of Islamic Republic Of Afghanistan, Kabul. http://www.embassyofafghanistan.org/sites/default/files/publications/Afghanistan_National_Development_Strategy_eng.pdf

Kumar, A, 2010, A Review of Human Development Trends in South Asia: 1990-2009, Human Development Research Paper 2010/44, UNDP, Research Paper 2010/44
http://hdr.undp.org/sites/default/files/hdrp_2010_44.pdf

National Geographic, n.d, Education: Atoll
http://education.nationalgeographic.com/education/encyclopedia/atoll/?ar_a=1

National Planning Commission, 2013, An Approach Paper To The Thirteenth Plan (Fy 2013/14 – 2015/16)-Unofficial Translation, National Planning Commission, Kathmandu, Nepal.
http://www.npc.gov.np/new/uploadedFiles/allFiles/typeng13.pdf

Online Currency Convertor, n.d, United States dollar (USD) and Indian rupee (INR) Year 2005 Exchange Rate History - Yahoo Finance.
http://www.freecurrencyrates.com/exchange-rate-history/USD-INR/2005

Patel. V and R, Shidhaye, n.d, Depression, South Asia Network for Chronic Disease, Gurgaon, Haryana
http://sancd.org/uploads/pdf/Depression_fact_sheet.pdf

Planning Commission, 2007, Pakistan in the 21st Century, Vision 2030, Planning Commission, Government of Pakistan, Islamabad,
www.pc.gov.pk/vision2030/Pak21stcentury/vision%202030-Full.pd

Planning Commission, 2011, Sixth Five Year Plan FY2011-FY2015, Accelerating Growth and Reducing Poverty, Part-II, Sectoral Strategies, Programmes and Policies, Planning Commission, Government of the People's *Republic of Bangladesh* http://www.plancomm.gov.bd/wp-content/uploads/2013/09/SFYP_Part-2.pdf

Planning Commission, 2013, Twelfth Five Year Plan (2012–2017) Social Sectors, Volume III, Planning Commission, Government of India, New Delhi, www.planningcommission.gov.in/plans/planrel/12thplan/pdf/12fyp_vol3.pdf

Royal Government of Bhutan, 2013, Eleventh Five Year Plan Volume II: Programme Profile, 2013-2018, Self-reliance and Inclusive Green Socio-economic Development, Gross National Happiness Commission, Royal Government of Bhutan, Thimpu. http://www.gnhc.gov.bt/wp-content/uploads/2011/04/11th-Plan-Vol-2.pdf

The Guardian, Saturday 8th March 2014, Nepal's CHAUPADI tradition banishes menstruating women – in pictures http://www.theguardian.com/global-development/gallery/2014/mar/08/nepal-chaupadi-tradition-banishes-menstruating-women-in-pictures

United Nations, n.da, Status as at : 27-05-2014 08:04:19 EDT Chapter IV Human Rights g. Convention on the Elimination of All Forms of Discrimination against Women https://treaties.un.org/Pages/ViewDetails.aspx?src=TREATY&mtdsg_no=IV-8&chapter=4&lang=en

United Nations, n.db, United Nations Treaty Collection STATUS AS AT : 21-05-2014 08:11:58 EDT, CHAPTER IV HUMAN RIGHTS: 8 .b Optional Protocol to the Convention on the Elimination of All Forms of Discrimination against Women, https://treaties.un.org/Pages/ViewDetails.aspx?src=TREATY&mtdsg_no=IV-8-b&chapter=4&lang=en

United Nations, n.dc, Maldives Abortion Policy, www.un.org/esa/population/publications/abortion/doc/maldives.doc

United Nations, n.dd, India Abortion Policy,
www.un.org/esa/population/publications/abortion/doc/india.doc

United Nations, n.de, Convention on the Elimination of All Forms of Discrimination against Women, Country Reports, http://www.un.org/womenwatch/daw/cedaw/reports.htm

United Nations Children's Fund, n.d Introduction to the Convention on the Rights of the Child: Definition of key terms , www.unicef.org/crc/files/Definitions.pdf

United Nations Development Programme, 2013, Human Development Report 2013 The Rise of the South: Human Progress in a Diverse World http://hdr.undp.org/sites/default/files/reports/14/hdr2013_en _complete.pdf

United Nations Children's Fund (UNICEF), n.d, Water, Environment and Sanitation, UNICEF-India, New Delhi http://www.unicef.org/india/wes.html

United Nations Population Division, n.d, Sex Ratio at Birth, http://data.un.org/Data.aspx?d=PopDiv&f=variableID%3A5 2

UN Women n.da, The Convention on the Elimination of All Forms of Discrimination Against Women, http://www.un.org/womenwatch/daw/cedaw/text/econventio n.htm

United Nations Women, n.db, Convention on the Elimination of All Forms of Discrimination against Women, Reservations to CEDAW, http://www.un.org/womenwatch/daw/cedaw/reservations.ht m

Women on Waves, n.da, Nepal,
http://www.womenonwaves.org/en/search?qs=Nepal

Women on Waves, n.db, Afghanistan
http://www.womenonwaves.org/en/search?qs=Afghanistan

Women on Waves, n.dc, Sri Lanka,
http://www.womenonwaves.org/en/page/2725/sri-lanka

Women on Waves, n.dd, Bangladesh,
http://www.womenonwaves.org/en/search?qs=bangladesh

Women on Waves, n.de, Pakistan
http://www.womenonwaves.org/en/search?qs=Pakistan

Women on Waves, n.df, Bhutan,
http://www.womenonwaves.org/en/search?qs=Bhutan

Women on waves, n.dg, India
http://www.womenonwaves.org/en/page/2731/india

World Economic Forum, 2013, Insight Report, Global Gender Gap Report 2013, World Economic Forum, Switzerland.
http://www3.weforum.org/docs/WEF_GenderGap_Report_2013.pdf

World Health Organisation, n.da, Investing in Health: A Summary of the Findings of the Commission on Macroeconomics and Health, CMH Unit, World Health Organisation, Geneva
http://www.who.int/macrohealth/infocentre/advocacy/en/investinginhealth02052003.pdf

World Health Organisation, n.db, Tough Choices: Investing in Health for Development, Questions and Answers, http://www.who.int/macrohealth/documents/Q&A%20final.

pdf?ua=1

World Health Organisation, 2007, Women's health and human rights: Monitoring the implementation of CEDAW, World Health Organisation, Geneva

World Health Organisation, 2009, World Health Statistics, Table , Health workforce, infrastructure, essential medicines, http://www.who.int/whosis/whostat/EN_WHS09_Table6.pdf

World Health Organisation, 2013, World Health Statistics 2013, Part III: Global Health Indicators, World Health Organisation, Geneva , http://www.who.int/gho/publications/world_health_statistics/EN_WHS2013_Part3.pdf

www.ingramcontent.com/pod-product-compliance
Lightning Source LLC
Chambersburg PA
CBHW070123290526
45789CB00005B/2127